Alana Ziaya
1606 E Fillmore St.
Marshfield, WI 54449

style to go Home Solutions

D1512218

style to go

Home Solutions

JOSH GARSKOF

The Taunton Press

Text © 2007 by The Taunton Press, Inc.
All rights reserved.

The Taunton Press
Inspiration for hands-on living®

The Taunton Press, Inc., 63 South Main Street,
PO Box 5506, Newtown, CT 06470-5506
e-mail: tp@taunton.com

Jacket/Cover design: Allison Wilkes
Interior design: Kimberly Adis, Allison Wilkes
Layout: Cathy Cassidy

Library of Congress Cataloging-in-Publication Data
Garskof, Josh.
  Style to go-- home solutions / Josh Garskof.
     p. cm.
  ISBN-13: 978-1-56158-932-6
  ISBN-10: 1-56158-932-2
  1. Storage in the home. 2. House furnishings. 3. Interior
decoration. I. Title. II. Title: Style to go. III. Title: Home
solutions.

TX309.G37 2007
648'.8--dc22

                                        2006020159

Printed in China
10 9 8 7 6 5 4 3 2 1

The following manufacturers/names appearing in *Home Solutions* are
trademarks: Alkco® Lighting, American Standard®, Bed, Bath & Beyond®,
Blanco®, California Closets®, Casabella®, Chicago Faucets®, ClosetMaid®,
Corian®, Country Floors®, Dacor®, Elkay®, Exposures®, Filofax®, Franke®
Sinks & Faucets, Freedom Bag®, Frigidaire®, Frontgate®, General Electric®,
Halo® Lighting, Hold Everything®, Ikea®, Jenn-Air®, KitchenAid®,Kmart®,
Kohler® Plumbing, Kraftmaid®, Levenger®, Lightolier®, Maytag®,Moen®,
PEZ®, Restoration Hardware℠, Rubbermaid®, Target®,Thermador®,
Tupperware®, Umbra®, Viking®, Wicanders® Cork Flooring, Wolf®

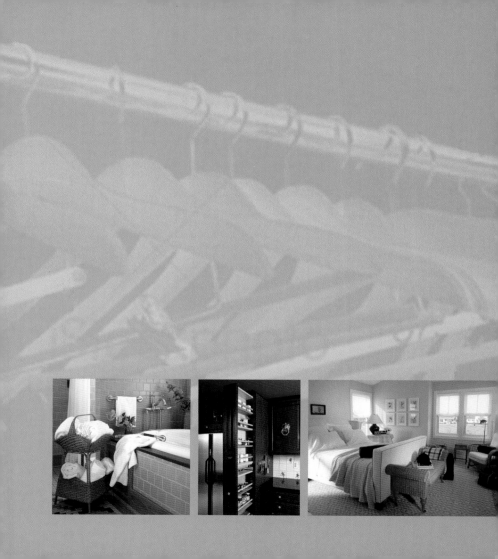

contents

around
the house

If you have young children, consider replacing your coffee table with an oversized ottoman. It'll provide a softer landing for adventuresome youngsters, extra seating for large gatherings, and even an impromptu spot for changing diapers.

If you want to hide your media equipment inside an armoire but can't justify the cost of a big piece of furniture, use simple utility shelving made of wire or wood and dress it up with standard tab-top curtains.

Trade multiple
remote controls
for a single
"universal" type
that will operate all
audio and
video equipment

Top Tame the maze of cords behind TVs, stereos, and computers with a flexible plastic tube that has a slit along its length that allows you to stuff wires inside.

Bottom Next time you plug a bunch of cords into a power strip, label each one first using a standard office label.

Create one-of-a-kind displays in your house by collecting and displaying whatever interests you, from PEZ® candy dispensers to antique glassware to snow globes; it's amazing what you can find at yard sales and auction websites.

Store your photos
and music digitally
on a computer
and you can move
those bulky CDs
and photo boxes
into long-term storage.

Below left Tired of staring at those giant racks that hold your ever-growing CD collection? Use them as drawer liners to keep all of your music out of sight yet still easily accessible.

Below right Attach library-style drawer pulls to help better identify what's inside cabinet drawers. Print label inserts from the computer to keep the look tidy.

A LOT OF THINGS WE
NEVER USE
(BUT STILL CAN'T THROW AWAY)

Displaying your children's artwork is a great way to inspire their creativity and fill your walls with an ever changing gallery of original art. Hang the works in store-bought frames or just pin them to a decorative bulletin board.

Wood and metal
radiator covers are available
in a host of sizes and styles.

Not only do radiator covers dress up clunky old-fashioned radiators—which can be hard to keep clean—but they also can prevent burns and actually improve heating efficiency by directing heat away from windows.

Most homes have nooks and crannies just waiting to be turned into usable living space, like a desk area under the stairs.

Add a serving tray to the top of an ottoman to provide a safe adult serving space and storage for books and the TV remote.

Right Layering on two different colors of paint and then rubbing portions of the top coat away before it dries gave this simple table an antique look.

Below A mismatched table and chairs have been given a unifying theme with a freehand floral decorating scheme, which could just as easily have come from stencils purchased at an arts and crafts store.

A little paint
is all it takes to
transform boring
furniture
into the showpieces
of your home.

Left This narrow piece of carpet didn't cost a lot of money and launched the idea of turning an ordinary playroom into a kid's dream space.

Opposite Painting a floor is far less costly than purchasing carpeting—and far easier to keep clean, too. A couple of coats of polyurethane help to protect the paint from scratches and nicks.

Leave wainscot natural
to provide relief for bare walls.
But color the panels
or the trim
to draw attention to the wall
and frame a space.

Left Beadboard plywood can be purchased in 4 x 8 sheets and installed end to end around a room, creating an instant wainscot.

Below Aside from paint, the two-tone wainscot is made from nothing more than boards called furring strips that are installed at regular intervals and topped with another strip and a molding.

Above Put any empty wall space to use by adding shelving units. Easy-to-install wire shelves are perfect for a laundry room. Look for ready-to-assemble types for a more finished look.

Left A wraparound display case created from modular cubbies and topped off with crown molding makes the most of an empty wall.

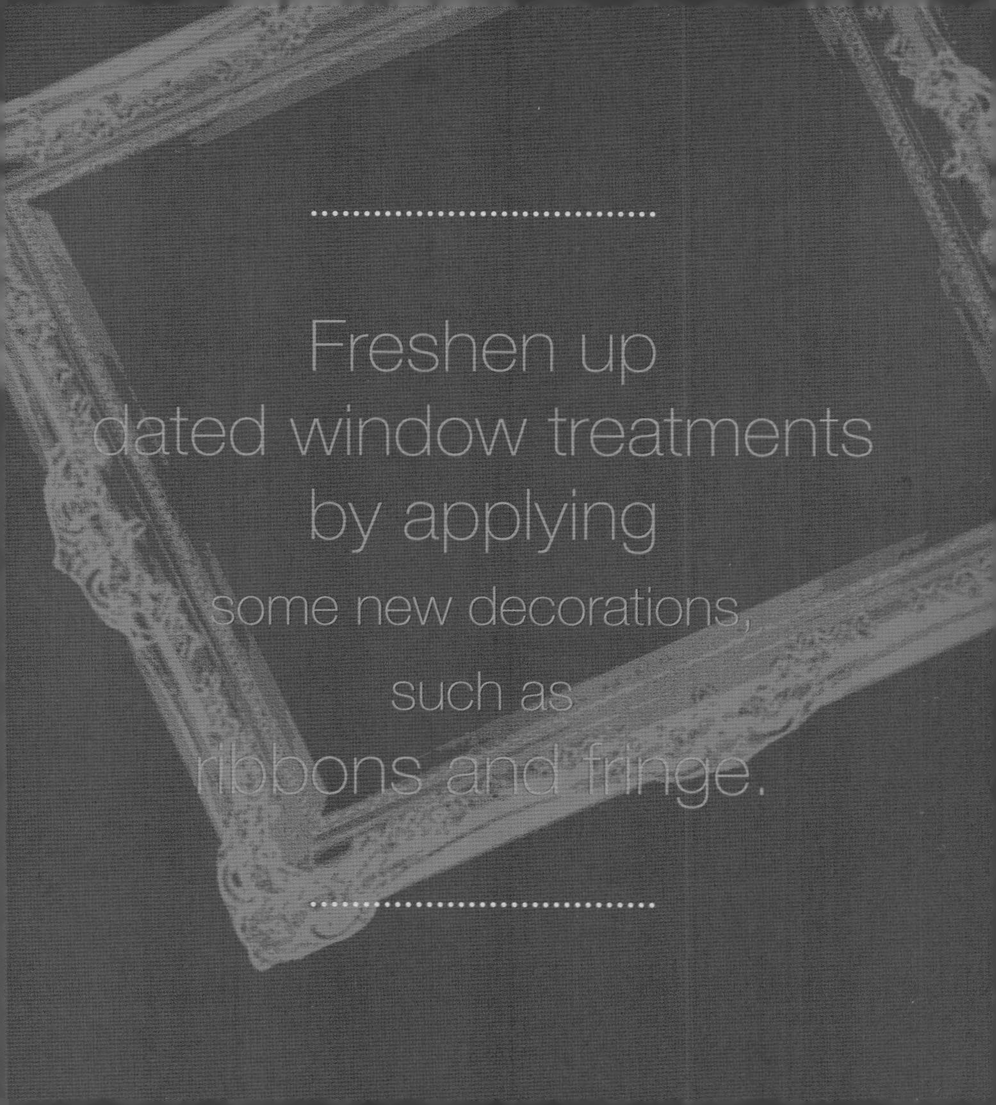

·····················

Freshen up
dated window treatments
by applying
some new decorations,
such as
ribbons and fringe.

·····················

Make a room grow
with your child
by repainting a cornice
or applying a collage
of wallpaper cutouts
to change the theme
of the room quickly
and inexpensively.

Above Guest beds can double as comfortable seating when pillows are covered and arranged along the back.

Right Slipcovers instantly transform furniture. This set has a pattern that's more suitable for winter months, so white slipcovers make them just right for spring and summer. You can order stock covers in standard sizes from many furnishings catalogs.

A new light fixture
can brighten any space.
It can stand out and add
style or blend in and
add pratical value.

kitchens

Short on cabinet space? Make the most of your cabinets by installing dividers that allow you to fill every inch and still easily get what you want without having to shuffle other items out of the way.

Before painting cabinets, **remove hinges, knobs, and shelves** and scrub greasy spots with painters' detergent.

Left Cabinet pulls come in hundreds of styles from slim to bulky, mod to retro, sophisticated to quirky.

Opposite New kitchen cabinets cost a fortune, but you can make your old ones look new with a couple of coats of paint and a new set of knobs and pulls.

It's hard to get at the stuff stored far inside a deep cabinet, unless you install one of the many kits available for making access easier, from sliding bins to pull-out shelves to lazy Susans.

Above and right Poor lighting in your kitchen? Here's a simple solution: Add under-cabinet lighting. You don't even have to hire an electrician to run any wiring if you install battery-operated units.

Left For odd-shaped spaces, try rope lighting, which can snake around corners. It comes by the foot or in precut lengths.

Left Knife storage doesn't have to mean a bulky block on the counter. Magnetic strips keep knives handy and out of reach of small fingers.

Right Here's a space-saving way to store spices: Load them in metal canisters and hang them from the magnetic strips sold for storing knives.

Take a cue from restaurants and hang pots and pans from a pot rack, rail, or hooks. This solution keeps them stored but readily available.

If you have the space, try storing your plastic food containers with their lids on top, and you'll never have to go searching for the right container and lid combination again.

Help wooden kitchen
gear to last longer
by seasoning it
with a few drops of
food-grade mineral oil
before each of
the first few uses
and then occasionally
over the life of the item.

Opposite Snap-top glass canisters keep dry goods fresher than their original packages, and they turn staples and snacks into works of art.

Top left Prevent dishes from moving around when the drawer gets opened and shut by adding wooden pegs to the drawer bottom.

Bottom left Cabinet inserts will raise items on the back of the shelf so you can more easily see and reach the supplies that can otherwise hide back there.

One of the best ways to make a kitchen organized is to keep things you use daily within reach but hidden away.

Wire furniture is a cost-effective way
to add storage and give the kitchen
a professional look.

Don't be afraid to let your cooking implements be seen. Here, spoons, spatulas, and tongs have been arranged into bouquets and displayed in a set of attractive pitchers right behind a peninsula cooktop.

Never use an abrasive
scouring pad on
a nonstick pan
because it could scratch
the coating.
Instead, look for a gentle,
non-scratching product.

An inside-the-sink shelf, which attaches with strong suction cups, eliminates the drips and mess of storing sponges and soaps on the back rim of the sink.

Basket drawers are ideal for storing foods such as potatoes and onions, which benefit from having a free flow of air around them to keep them fresh. They work pretty well for crayons, too.

Place a child-size desk, a beanbag reading corner, or an arts and crafts station near your kitchen so your kids can entertain themselves while you cook.

Here are two secrets
to an organized junk drawer:
Use dividers to keep
loose items separate,
and use heavy-duty
full-extension glides
so you can access
the whole drawer.

You can turn any surface
or two of chalk-board paint,

The text on the chalkboard door reads:

grocery
salad dressing flour
bread onions
dove bars soap
goat cheese
greek olives
limeade
milk

dates
greg. 9/22 6:30
dentist Jeff 9:30
Ravinia 9/29
Steak Fry 9/17
photos 9/24

Jim—to do!
Frame Pics
Book Hotel
Clean garage
Sunday: L Zurich 9:45 AM

Rachael
Tonya/Marisa party 9/29
downtown w/ Dad 9/20

Make appetizer for Sat. nite!

I LOVE YOU

To DAD LOVE RACHAEL

Left This door's glass has been replaced with steel panels that have a chalk board finish, and each square has a specific purpose—to-do lists, phone messages, shopping lists, and artwork held in place by magnets.

Opposite The simplest family message center you can get is a chalk board that's hung where everyone will see it, such as above a coat rack.

into a chalk board with a coat available at home centers.

Designate one spot
in your kitchen,
no matter
how small, to function
as the dropping place for
daily mail, keys, laptop,
and rechargeable phone.

Use a tray under your dish drying rack to contain water that runs off your dishes (left), or you can order a new countertop with a built-in drainboard (above).

Morning time is typically chaotic in any kitchen, especially when you're half asleep. Relegate coffee fixins, the toaster oven, and other things used on a daily basis to their own spot in the kitchen.

Improve traffic flow
in your kitchen
by identifying the busiest
work zones
and relocating them
around the perimeter
of the room.

Every household needs a few colorful serving trays. These underappreciated tools look great whether they're displayed on a countertop (above) or hard at work on a dining room buffet (left).

bedrooms
& closets

For a quick room
makeover, change the
position of the elements.
Placing a bed on an
angle will give it
more presence.

Above In a small bedroom, nightstands can serve multiple functions. On one side of this bed, nesting tables can be moved anywhere in the room as needed. On the other, a writing desk doubles as a nightstand.

Left This two-drawer dresser is big enough to serve as a nightstand for two guest beds.

Right Add a fringed skirt to a simple table to turn it into striking nightstand.

Below The bench at the foot of this tall bed provides visual interest in the room—and also a convenient place to sit when getting dressed.

Buy unfinished furniture

and do the painting

or staining yourself.

You'll pay a fraction of the cost

of standard

furniture-store prices.

Above Want to be a little adventurous in painting? Use stencils to add detail on a wall, ceiling, or even a floor.

Right Sticky-backed wall art is available from home stores and many online sources. Using these decals is a great way to add a theme to a room.

Even a small bedroom benefits from a chair. When pulled up to a desk (opposite) or placed in a corner (left) the chair will neither be tripped over nor a dumping ground for yesterday's outfit.

Above When bedroom space is tight, consider a sliding closet door, which eliminates the need for a door to swing into the room and take up precious space.

Left Many houses have unused spaces inside some walls that can easily become built-in shelves.

Above left Not only are plastic clothes hangers gentler on fabrics than the standard wire ones, they're also less prone to tangling, which makes for a neater closet.

Above right Tame your unruly dresser drawers by outfitting them with plastic dividers sold at office supply stores.

Opposite Hanging a few wall hooks or pegs around the perimeter of the room provides convenient storage for everything from hats to sweatshirts to bathrobes.

Ready-made closet kits are a lot cheaper than custom closet systems, and they're extremely effective in helping you to organize your closet.

Above A closet is the perfect place for a built-in dresser.

Left Pullout wire cubbies are a great way to organize clothes by type, color, or season.

Far left Shoe bags are underrated. One with clear fronts helps children find their own shoes. They're also great for storing dolls and action figures.

Arrange a child's closet
so that rods and shelves
are at eye level.

Left Roll-around storage bins make cleanup quicker. Those made of light yet durable construction are easiest for kids to use.

Right A small shelving unit at the bottom of a closet provides a place for toys, games, sports equipment, and books. It's top is a perfect place for shoes.

kids' spaces

An alcove under the stairs takes on new life as a reading corner stocked with plenty of comfy pillows and soft lighting.

Infuse your child's room with color and personality by painting a dresser or wardrobe. You could even let your child help create a more abstract-painted version.

Painting a play room floor will give you the design appeal of colorful carpeting—but with a flatter surface that's better for supporting toys and games and that's easier to keep clean.

Over-the-door shoe caddies and seat-back car organizers are soft and washable and they keep baby toys and gear neat and accessible. You can even decorate them with fabric remnants.

Be creative when looking for ways to store toys and games. Some of the best storage products aren't even intended for toys.

Store-bought **hanging shelves are colorful, quick to install, and immediately add visual interest** and display space to the room—while keeping breakable items out of reach of tiny fingers.

Don't let the space under the crib go to waste. Purchase wire baskets that are sized to fit underneath the lowest mattress setting, and use a crib skirt to partially hide them from view while allowing you to quickly spot what you're looking for.

Bookcases can hold a lot more than books. The best also offer room to store games and toys, and plenty of space to get things on and off easily.

Make it easy
for kids to store
their own toys
by giving them each a
storage bin labeled
with their name
or the toys that
belong inside.

If space or money is tight, you don't need a dedicated changing table for a baby nursery. The top of a low dresser or shelving unit will do the job, as long as it has a lip around the edge or a strap-on belt to keep the baby safe.

Above Stock your playroom with plenty of labeled bins and you'll always know where each toy belongs.

Right Label a hanging sweater organizer with the days of the week and stock it with complete outfits so your youngster can dress himself each morning, learn the days of the week—and always wear clothes that match.

If your kids don't read yet,
make toy labels
from a clip art website.

Bedding and artwork are easy to change as your child's interests and sense of style mature—or as your children change bedrooms. Paint and furniture aren't so easy to change, so it's a good idea to let the decorating theme come from the temporary details.

Liven up kids' furniture with whimsical knobs, which can be easily replaced at any time.

Opposite Stackable plastic bins are ideal for toy storage since they're easy to clean, are softer than wood or metal, and come in a rainbow of bright colors.

Left Stylish storage doesn't have to be expensive. Basic wire kitchen shelving becomes an attractive armoire when it's wrapped with a fabric cover complete with storage pockets.

Opposite Organize a
child's desk the same way
you would your own, with
drawer dividers for sup-
plies and hanging folders
for projects. It'll encourage
her to keep things tidy and
give her an early lesson in
good study habits.

Right and below A group
of small plastic bins keeps
small items organized in a
child's drawer.

Left Colorful unused flowerpots make eye-catching desktop containers for markers and other art supplies.

Below Though it's most often used in garages and basements, pegboard can also be an attractive, low-cost and kid-friendly way to keep toys, dolls, and books organized.

When choosing
a storage system for kids,
look for one that can
grow with your child
and be reconfigured easily
as needs change.

Create the ultimate storage area on the cheap by using ready-to-assemble components, which you can find at home centers and home stores.

Above This desk was created by installing a simple desktop and wall-hung shelf in an unused alcove.

Left Modular storage units are ideal for children's rooms because you can rearrange them to accommodate the youngsters' changing toys, interests, and reach.

Whether they're in a closet or a freestanding armoire, children's clothes don't require much hanging space, so you can install shelving just a couple of feet below the closet pole.

Removable
wall decals
bring a fanciful look
to kid spaces
that you can easily
take down when
the children get older.

A child-sized coat rack
and some beach pails
can become a unique
toy dispenser.

Above Rickrack shelves—
which are nothing more than
1-ft. boards nailed and glued in
a zigzag pattern—are simple to
make and work as CD storage.

Left Once your child is old
enough let them use magnets
to hang up notes and keep track
of library books, parties,
and school events.

The best
toy bins let kids
see their belongings
even as they keep them
organized and
out of the way.

Right Take a cue from a great kitchen storage idea and hide a laundry hamper inside a kid's room cabinet.

Left and below If space is tight, look for storage that doubles as a comfortable bench.

Bold colors

make playrooms feel lively
and child-like and
**can inspire
youngsters'
creativity.**

Window guards are a must for spaces where kids
will play alone and the windows are accessible.

Things
TO DO

MAKE BED
PICK UP COATS
FEED DOG

Get kids involved in creating their own décor. Fabric-wrapped cork boards are easy-to-make photo and art galleries.

Any kid will love his own dedicated playroom, and converting an attic into one is a great use of space, especially since the lower ceiling height accomodates small people.

Make any play area really work by
leaving open space for floor play and
using furniture sized just for kids.

bathrooms

Pedestal sinks look great, but they don't offer much counter space. Supplement yours with a glass shelf, which is sturdy and easy to clean.

When hanging a shelf—or any heavy item—make sure that you fasten it to the wood framing in the wall.

Adding a shelf to the top of a wood wainscot provides extra storage or display space. A simple shelf over this bathtub displays decorative canisters that have been loaded with bath supplies.

Opposite Always mount hooks for hand towels right over the sink so guests can quickly find them without dripping on the floor.

Left Having trouble keeping track of whose towel is whose? Try assigning each family member his own towel hook—or his own towel color.

A collection of beach finds can turn your bathroom from ho-hum
to fun—and remind you of the places you've been.

Keep your bathroom mirror
from fogging up
by using the products
sold at auto-supply stores
for keeping your car's windshield
from doing the same.

Fresh towels need not be hidden away in a linen closet. Stack them out in the open, and look for interesting ways to display them, such as an antique wicker plant stand (left) or a wall-mounted wire basket (right).

Above Any tub that has lost its luster can become new again with an acrylic liner. This is essentially a new tub and wall surround that gets custom molded for your bathroom and installed right over the existing tub.

Right An old clawfoot tub takes on new life when its underside is painted with fanciful stripes.

Freestanding furniture in nearly any style can provide supplemental bathroom storage—as long as it's made from water-resistant materials.

Right and below Looking for a little extra bathroom storage? Convert unused space inside your walls into built-in shelving for your bathroom.

Plastic caddies make it easy to get what you need before stepping into the shower.

bathrooms

You can make a compact bathroom feel more spacious with a retractable curtain rod that moves out of the way when it's not in use.

Unfitted
cabinetry can
fit perfectly
in a
bathroom.

For any bathroom
that kids will use,
make sure to select
only sturdy shelves,
and to keep adult
supplies out of reach.

Install multiple lights
help eliminate shadows

Update your bathroom by switching out light fixtures. Just be sure that the new fixture's base is at least as large as the old one so that it'll cover the wall opening.

in a bathroom to
when looking in the mirror.

Two sinks require two lights in order to illuminate both work areas—
and both people.

entries & mudrooms

With a storage bench, overhead cubby, umbrella stand, and cookie sheets to double as wet-shoe holders, this entry-way is sure to stay clean of clutter.

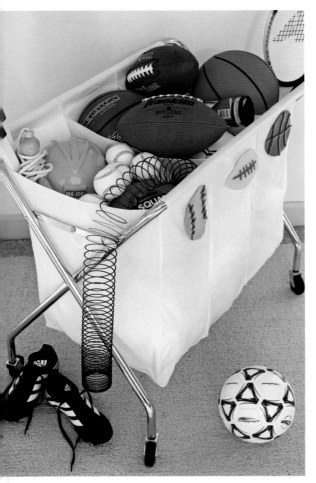

Opposite This storage area is pretty low-tech, with plywood boxes hung on the wall for storage cubes. They do the trick, though, by corralling all types of sports accessories.

Left Keep sports gear organized and out of the way by stowing it inside a laundry sorting cart.

An easy-to-clean floor is a must in any entryway that will see a lot of traffic. Tile is a good choice, as is linoleum, stone, or well-protected wood since all can be swept up and damp-mopped in no time.

A well-used hallway needs a place
to sit down and change boots,
shoes, and slippers.

No mudroom?
No problem. Convert
a couple of kitchen
cabinets that are by
the backdoor into
storage cubbies
for outdoor gear.

Make every entry welcoming by providing an insight into your personality with artwork, knick-knacks, and other décor.

This entryway is especially welcoming due to the soft light, subdued wall color, and expansive bench. It's also a great spot to wait for guests to arrive.

Top Doubling as a pantry, this mudroom is the perfect spot to drop off bags from the grocery store or backpacks when kids arrive home from school.

Bottom A bulletin board or chalkboard is a great addition to any mudroom. This one has both, making it all the more useful for keeping the family's comings and goings on track.

··

Expand your storage space by hanging wall shelves

in a back hall, utility closet,

basement stairwell, garage,

or breezeway.

··

home
workspaces

Turn an underused closet into a home office. The best part—close the door to hide the clutter.

If drawer space is scarce, hang your supplies and projects on the wall. Magnetic strips sold for hanging kitchen knives can hold metal canisters filled with supplies; magazine racks can serve as incoming and outgoing baskets.

All financial records
should be kept
for at least seven years.
Use a portable hanging file
folder box for each year,
label the outside,
and stack it
in a safe place.

28

Me Day

087   AT-A-GLANCE®   278

**Friday
March**

12:30 — Lunch at
with Susan

Protect yourself from identity theft

by shredding all trash that contains account numbers and financial data.

Opposite and above If your desk is in a spot where guests will see it, turn your supplies into a decorating asset by organizing them into glass canisters or arranging them in colorful serving trays.

Right Use small craft boxes to keep office supplies orderly in a desk drawer.

Locate the family computer in a public space so you can keep an eye on what games your kids are playing, what websites they're surfing, and how much time they're spending on the computer.

A retractable tray allows for a keyboard and mouse—or an entire laptop—to stow away under any countertop, desk, or work surface.

The two essentials for any functional desk are plenty of surface area and a height of about 30 in. off the floor. Here, a simple wooden slab is supported by two sawhorses.

To reduce clutter, scan medical and financial statements into your computer, index them electronically, and back them all up on DVD or CD.

Above You don't need a whole extra room to create a great home office. With today's ever shrinking technology, you can fit everything you need into an armoire or a closet.

Right Any space can be used for an office if you give it a desk with ample room.

Every laundry area needs a pole where freshly clean clothes can hang to dry or just to stay wrinkle free. Mounting it over a sink means wet clothes will drip right over the drain.

laundry & hobby spaces

Get your kids to take the first step toward laundry independence by giving them their own laundry basket cubbies—color coded for dirty and clean clothes—where they can deliver and pick up their stuff.

Above Traditional apothecary jars are as beautiful as they are useful when you use them to store essential laundry supplies.

Right An attractive and comfortable laundry closet makes the hard work of washing and drying and folding the family's clothes feel just a little less like an unending chore.

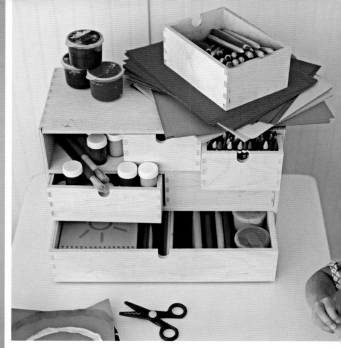

Above Keep arts and crafts supplies in age-appropriate containers so that kids work with just what you want them to.

Left Mounting rolled paper to a wall is a great way to eliminate the need for an easel. It also keeps floor space open for other activities.

laundry & hobby spaces

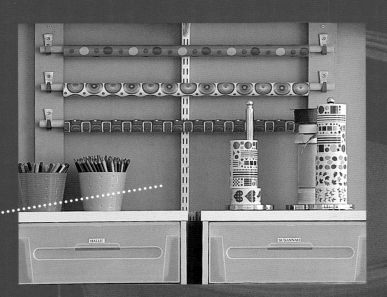

Dedicate a space in a
spare bedroom or the
basement for an arts
and crafts or wrapping
center where family
members can go to do
various projects.

Whether
you have a sewing
basket or a whole
sewing station,
the laundry room
is a great place
to stow
your sewing gear.

garages

Don't throw away old cabinets and countertops when you remodel your kitchen; instead give them new life as a workbench where you can store tools and do projects.

When organizing the garage, think about creating different zones for different categories of belongings. Give sports equipment, car cleaning supplies, summer gear, and tools their own own space.

Screw a wireless light adapter into any porch or breezeway light fixture and you'll be able to turn it on from a remote control in your car or on your keychain.

Turn your garage into a mudroom by placing some stackable wooden toy cubbies by the door leading into the house. Add a bench if there's space.

Install 1x 2 wood strips on the wall and add some screws to use as hangers to create a basic garage tool station.

Buy a can of spray paint
in your favorite color and
put a spot on each
of your tools,
so you'll always know
which are yours.

garages

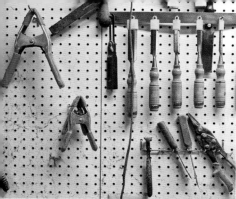

Pegboard (left) is a decidedly low tech solution for storing tools—and it works great. But it's not the only option. If you want to hang heavy-duty yard tools, think about a wall panel system (below) or a wall-mounted wire rack (opposite).

sources

organizations

American Institute
of Architects (AIA)
1735 New York Ave. NW
Washington, DC 200006
www.aiaaccess.com

American Society of
Interior Designers (ASID)
608 Massachusetts Ave. NE
Washington, DC 20002
www.interiors.org

National Association of
Home Builders (NAHB)
1201 Fifteenth St. NW
Washington, DC 20005
www.nahb.org

National Association of
Professional Organizers
www.napo.net

National Association of the
Remodeling Industry (NARI)
4900 Seminary Road #3210
Alexandria, VA 22311
www.nari.org

National Kitchen & Bath
Association
687 Willow Grove St.
Hackettstown, NJ 07840
www.nkba.com

web sites

Decorating Den Interiors
www.decoratingden.com

Dr. Toy
www.drtoy.com

Energy Star
www.energystar.com/gov

Get Decorating
www.GetDecorating.com

HomePortfolio
www.homeportfolio.com

The Building and Home
Improvement Directory
www.build.com

U.S. Consumer Product
Safety Commission
www.cpsc.gov

product sources

Alkco® Lighting
www.alkco.com

American Standard®
www.americanstandard.com

Babybox.com
www.babybox.com

Bed, Bath & Beyond®
www.bedbathandbeyond.com

Bernhardt Furniture
Company
www.bernhardt.com

Blanco®
www.blancoamerica.com

Broadway Panhandler
www.broadwaypanhandler.com

Broyhill Furniture
Industries, Inc.
www.broyhillfurn.com

California Closets®
www.californiaclosets.com

Casabella®
www.casabella.com

CD Storehouse
(800) 829-4203

Chicago Faucets®
www.chicagofaucets.com

Closet Factory
www.closetfactory.com

ClosetMaid®
www.closetmaid.com

The Conran Shop
www.conran.com

The Container Store
www.containerstore.com

Corian®
www.corian.com

Crate & Barrel
www.crateandbarrel.com

Country Floors®
www.countryfloors.com

Dacor®
www.dacor.com

Design Within Reach
www.dwr.com

Elkay®
www.elkayusa.com

Exposures®
www.exposuresonline.com

Filofax®
www.filofax.com

Franke® Sinks & Faucets
www.frankeksd.com

Freedom Bag®
www.freedombag.com

Frigidaire®
www.frigidaire.com

Frontgate®
www.frontgate.com

General Electric®
www.geappliances.com

Graber Window Fashions
www.springs.com

Gracious Home
www.gracioushome.com

Harden Furniture, Inc.
www.harden.com

Halo® Lighting
www.cooperlighting.com

Hold Everything®
www.holdeverything.com

HomeDecInASec
www.homedecinasec.com

Ikea®
www.ikea.com

Jenn-Air®
www.jennair.com

KitchenAid®
www.kitchenaid.com

Kmart™
www.kmart.com

Knape & Vogt
www.knapeandvogt.com

Kohler® Plumbing
www.us.kohler.com

Kraftmaid®
www.kraftmaid.com

The Land of Nod
www.thelandofnod.com

Lamps Plus
www.lampsplus.com

Lane Home Furnishings
www.lanefurniture.com

Levenger®
www.levenger.com

Lightolier®
www.lightolier.com

Mannington, Inc.
www.mannington.com

Maytag®
www.maytag.com

Moen®
www.moen.com

Netkidswear.com
www.netkidswear.com

Poliform
www.poliformusa.com

Posh Tots
www.poshtots.com

Rejuvenation lighting
and hardware
www.rejuvenation.com

Restoration Hardware℠
www.restorationhardware.com

Rev-A-Shelf
www.rev-a-shelf.com

Rubbermaid®
www.rubbermaid.com

Seabrook Wallcoverings
www.seabrookwallcoverings.com

Serena & Lily
www.serenaandlily.com

Stacks and Stacks
www.stacksandstacks.com

Target®
www.target.com

Thermador®
www.thermador.com

Thomasville Furniture
Industries
www.thomasville.com

Tupperware®
www.tupperware.com

Umbra®
www.umbra.com

Velux America, Inc.
www.veluxusa.com

Vermont Soapstone
Company
www.vermontsoapstone.com

Viking®
www.vikingrange.com

WallCandy Arts
www.wallcandyarts.com

Wallies
www.wallies.com

The Warm Biscuit Bedding
Company
www.warmbiscuit.com

Wicanders® Cork Flooring
www.wicanders.com

Wolf®
www.subzero.com/wolf

York Wallcoverings
www.yorkwall.com

photo
credits

pp. ii-iii: Photo: © Eric Roth.

p. v: (left) Photo: © Rob Karosis; (middle) Photo: © Grey Crawford; (right) Photo: © Jessie Walker.

p. vi: (far left) Photo: © Eric Roth, Design: Weena & Spook; (left) Photo: © Melabee M. Miller; (middle) Photo: © Mark Samu, www.samustudios.com, Design: Lucianna Samu; (right) Photo: © Tim Street-Porter; (far right) Photo: © Wendell T. Webber.

p. 1: (far left) Photo: © Wendell T. Webber; (left and middle) Photos: © Roger Turk/Northlight Photography; (right) Photo: © John Rickard, © The Taunton Press, Inc.

CHAPTER 1

p. 3: Photo: © Eric Roth, Design: Weena & Spook.

pp. 4-5: Photo: © Philip Ennis.

p. 7: Photos: © Wendell T. Webber.

p. 8: (top) Photo: © www.davidduncanlivingston.com; (bottom) Photo: © Eric Roth, Design: Cindy Seely.

p. 9: Photo: © Eric Roth.

p. 11: (left) Photo: © Melabee M. Miller; (right) Photo: © Povy Kendal Atchison.

p. 12: Photo: © Steve Vierra, www.stevevierraphotography.com.

p. 13: Photo: courtesty Posh Tots.

p. 14: Photo: © Mark Samu/Hearst Specials.

p. 15: Photo: © Robert Perron.

p. 16: Photo: © Grey Crawford.

p. 17: Photo: © Mark Samu/Hearst Specials.

p. 18: (top) Photo: © Mark Samu, www.samustudios.com, Design: Lucianna Samu; (bottom) Photo: © Jessie Walker.

p. 20: Photo: © Jane Langmuir.

p. 21: Photo: © Michael Pennello Photography.

p. 23: Photos: © Brian Vanden Brink.

p. 24: Photo: © Norman McGrath.

p. 25: Photo: © Mark Samu, www.samustudios.com

p. 26: Photo: © Lee Anne White, Design: Betty Romberg.

p. 28: (left) Photo: courtesy Wallies; (right) Photo: © Eric Roth.

p. 30: Photo: © Brian Vanden Brink.

p. 31: Photo: © www.davidduncanlivingston.com.

p. 32: (left) Photo: © Mark Samu, www.samustudios.com; (left) Photo: © Rob Karosis.

p. 33: (top) Photo: © Steve Vierra, www.stevevierraphotography.com; (bottom) Photo: © www.davidduncanlivingston.com.

CHAPTER 2

p. 35: Photo: © Melabee M. Miller.

p. 36: Photo: courtesy The Kennebec Company.

p. 37: Photo: courtesy Lee Valley Tools.

p. 38: Photo: © Ken Gutmaker.

p. 39: (top) Photo: Roe A. Osborn, © The Taunton Press, Inc.; (bottom) Photos: © Ken Gutmaker.

p. 40: Photo: © Ken Gutmaker.

p. 41: Photos: Christopher Bendetta, © The Taunton Press, Inc.

pp. 42-43: Photos: © Grey Crawford.

p. 44: Photo: © Golbus Cork.

p. 45: (top left) Photo: © Grey Crawford; (top right) Photo: Charles Miller, © The Taunton Press, Inc.; (bottom left) Photo: © Melabee M. Miller; (bottom right) Photo: 2006 Carolyn L. Bates, www.carolynlbates.com.

p. 46: Photo: © Robert Perron.

p. 48: Photo: © Eric Piasecki.

p. 49: (top) Photo: © Melabee M. Miller; (bottom) Photo: © Eric Roth.

pp. 50–51: Photos: © www.daviddun-canlivingston.com.

p. 52: Photo: © Tim Street-Porter.

p. 53: Photo: © Tim Street-Porter, Design: Martynus-Tripp, Inc.

p. 54: Photo: © Sandy Agrafiotis.

p. 57: Photo: © The Taunton Press, Inc., Design: Diane Morgan.

p. 58: Photo: © Eric Roth, Design: Weena & Spook.

pp. 59–60: Photos: Charles Miller, © The Taunton Press, Inc.

p. 62: Photo: Karen Tanaka, © The Taunton Press, Inc.

p. 63: Photo: Charles Miller, © The Taunton Press, Inc., Architect: James DeLuca.

p. 65: (left) Photo: © Ken Gutmaker; (right) Photo: © Chipper Hatter.

pp. 66–68: Photos: © Ken Gutmaker.

p. 70: Photo: © Eric Roth, Design: Weena & Spook.

p. 71: Photo: © Wendell T. Webber.

CHAPTER 3

p. 73: Photo: © Mark Samu, www.samustudios.com, Design: Lucianna Samu.

p. 74: Photo: © Brian Vanden Brink, Design: McMillan, Inc.

p. 75: Photo: Brian Vanden Brink, Design: Green Company Architects.

p. 76: (top) Photo: © www.daviddun-canlivingston.com; (bottom) Photo: © Jessie Walker.

p. 78: Photos: © David Bravo.

p. 79: Photo: courtesy York Wallcoverings.

pp. 80–81: Photos: Brian Vanden Brink.

p. 82: Photo: © Rob Karosis.

p. 83: Photo: © Ken Gutmaker.

p. 84: (left) Photo: Greg Premu, © The Taunton Press, Inc.; (right) Photo: © Wendell T. Webber.

p. 85: Photo: © Brian Vanden Brink.

p. 87: (top) Photo: courtesy Closet Maid; (bottom) Photo: © Wendell T. Webber.

p. 88: (left) Photo: © Wendell T. Webber; (right) Photo: © Robert Perron, Design: Killingworth.

p. 89: Photo: © Derrill Bazzy, Design: South Mountain Company.

p. 90: Photo: courtesy the Container Store.

p. 91: Photo: © Tim Street-Porter.

CHAPTER 4

p. 93: Photo: © Tim Street-Porter.

p. 94: Photo: © Beth Glbson.

p. 95: Photo: © www.davidduncanliv-ingston.com.

p. 96: Photo: © Wendell T. Webber.

p. 97: (left) Photo: © Wendell T. Webber; (right) Photo: courtesy Levels of Discovery.

p. 98: Photo: © Wendell T. Webber.

pp. 100–101: Photos: © Lisa Romerein.

p. 102: Photo: © Wendell T. Webber.

pp. 104–106: Photo: © Lisa Romerein.

p. 107: Photo: © Wendell T. Webber.

p. 108: Photos: © Wendell T. Webber, Design: John Loecke.

pp. 109–110: Photo: © Wendell T. Webber.

p. 111: Photo: courtesy The Land of Nod.

pp. 112–113: Photos: © Wendell T. Webber.

p. 114: (top) Photo: © Wendell T. Webber; (bottom) Photo: courtesy Georgia Pacific Corp.

p. 116: Photo: © Wendell T. Webber.

p. 117: Photo: © Steve Vierra, www.stevevierraphotography.com.

p. 118: Photo: © Wendell T. Webber.

p. 119: Photo: © Joshua McHugh, Design: Eileen Kasofsky.

p. 120: (top) Photo: courtesy Wall Candy Arts, www.wallcandyarts.com; (bottom) Photo: courtesy Wallies.

p. 122: Photo: courtesy The Warm Biscuit Bedding Company.

p. 123: (top) Photo: © Tria Giovan; (bottom) Photo: © Wendell T. Webber.

p. 124: (top left) Photo: courtesy Baby's Dream; (top right and bottom left) Photos: © Wendell T. Webber; (bottom right) Photo: courtesy The Land of Nod.

p. 126: Photo: © Wendell T. Webber.

p. 127: (top) Photo: courtesy California Closet, Inc.; (bottom) Photo: courtesy The Land of Nod.

p. 129: Photo: © Ricardo Moncada, Design: Victoria Benatar.

pp. 130–131: Photo: Todd Caverly, © Brian Vanden Brink Photography.

p. 132: Photo: © Douglas A. Salin, Design: Sherry Scott, ASID.

p. 133: Photo: © www.davidduncanlivingston.com.

pp. 134–135: Photo: © Tria Giovan.

CHAPTER 5

p. 137: Photo: © Wendell T. Webber.

p. 138: Photo: © Jason McConathy, Design: Kristin Dinner.

p. 139: Photo: © Philip Ennis.

p. 140: Photo: © Mark Samu, www.samustudios.com.

p. 141: Photo: © Melabee M. Miller.

p. 142: Photo: © Brian Vanden Brink.

p. 144: Photo: © Rob Karosis.

p. 145: Photo: © Philip Ennis, Design: Bradley, Klein, Thiergartner.

p. 146: Photo: Scott Gibson, © The Taunton Press, Inc.

p. 147: Photo: Charles Miller, © The Taunton Press, Inc., Design: Sheryl Murray-Hansen, Renovation Innovations.

p. 148: Photo: © Jeremey Samuelson.

p. 149: Photo: © Wendell T. Webber.

p. 150: (top) Photo: © Susan Kahn; (bottom) Photo: © Mark Samu, www.samustudios.com, Design: Val Florio Architects.

p. 151: Photo: Todd Caverly, © Brian Vanden Brink Photography.

pp. 152–153: Photos: © Grey Crawford, Design & Builder: Jim Garramone.

p. 154: Photo: © Brian Vanden Brink, Design: Schoz & Barclay Architects.

p. 155: Photo: © Wendell T. Webber.

pp. 156–157: Photos: Carl Weese, © The Taunton Press, Inc.

CHAPTER 6

p. 159: Photo: © Wendell T. Webber.

p. 160: Photo: © Eric Roth.

p. 161: Photo: © Wendell T. Webber.

p. 162: Photo: courtesy Glidden.

p. 163: Photo: © Jessie Walker.

p. 164: Photo: Randy O'Rourke, © The Taunton Press, Inc.

p. 165: Photo: © Brian Vanden Brink.

pp. 166–167: Photo: © Eric Roth.

p. 169: Photo: © www.davidduncanlivingston.com.

p. 170: (top) Photo: © www.davidduncanlivingston.com; (bottom) Photo: Randy O'Rourke, © The Taunton Press, Inc.

CHAPTER 7

p. 172: Photo: © Roger Turk/Northlight Photography.

p. 174: Photo: © Eric Piasecki.

p. 176: Photo: © Wendell T. Webber.

p. 177: Photos: © Eric Piasecki.

p. 179: (top) Photo: © Rob Karosis; (bottom) Photo: © www.davidduncan-livingston.com.

pp. 180–181: Photo: © Rob Karosis.

p. 182: Photo: © www.davidduncanliv-ingston.com.

p. 183: Photo: © Mark Samu, www.samustudios.com.

CHAPTER 8

p. 185: Photo: © Roger Turk/Northlight Photography.

pp. 186–187: Photos: © Rob Karosis.

p. 188: Photo: © Wendell T. Webber.

p. 189: Photo: courtesy Schulte Graphics Library.

p. 190: Photo: © Leslie Wright Dow, The Bainbridge Crew.

pp. 191–193: Photos: © Wendell T. Webber.

p. 195: (top) Photo: © Lee Anne White; (bottom) Photo: © Wendell T. Webber.

CHAPTER 9

pp. 197–199: Photo: John Rickard, © The Taunton Press, Inc.

p. 201: (top) Photo: John Rickard, © The Taunton Press, Inc.; (bottom) Photo: Jerry Bates, © The Taunton Press, Inc.

p. 202: Photo: © David Bravo.

p. 204: Photo: John Rickard, © The Taunton Press, Inc.

p. 205: (top) Photo: © Lee Anne White; (bottom) Photo: courtesy The Schulte Corporation.